FROM HIGHGATE TO HORNSEY

A Portrait in Old Picture Postcards

by
Ken Gay and Dick Whetstone

S.B. Publications
1989

CONTENTS

CONTENTS CONTINUED

CONTENTS CONTINUED

COVER ILLUSTRATION: Hornsey High Street, *c.*1915.
Is the soldier recruiting volunteers for the 1914 war? Shopkeeper 'P. Schwarz' is displaying the Union flag, probably to indicate his British loyalty, despite his German name. The memorial fountain, in obelisk form, was given to Hornsey Parish in 1863, and still survives, along with the adjacent drinking fountain and cattle trough but the buildings in the centre of the view have gone.

INTRODUCTION

Situated some five miles or so north of London, the Middlesex parish of Hornsey, now absorbed in the London Borough of Haringey, was still rural in the third quarter of the 19th century. The 1873 Ordnance Survey map shows little urban development, with fields and open spaces still dividing the village centres of Hornsey, Crouch End, Muswell Hill and Highgate. Settlement tended to be in the form of villas and small estates for prosperous Londoners who wanted a convenient retirement home in the countryside.

Highgate with its hill-top location, on the boundary of Hornsey parish, served by main roads out of London, was somewhat different. It had been favoured by the aristocracy in Tudor times and was to remain always a desirable area, sought by the wealthy as a near-London abode. It had, and still retains, the character of a small country town.

From the 1870s onwards, with the aid of rail transport and under pressure of population expansion as London's economic activites increased, the scene rapidly began to change. To the south, Islington, Hackney and other areas had already been extensively built over and Hornsey in turn began to be covered by terraced streets. In 1861 the census showed 11,082 people lived in the parish of about four square miles. By 1901 there were 72,056 and in 1903 Hornsey became a borough.

The terraced roads tended to be of substantial houses, designed for business people and clerks who worked in the capital. There was little local industry and local working class people tended to be in domestic service and in small workshops. Development across the parish was uneven and some parts, such as the Priory Road area and Muswell Hill, were not built up till early in the 20th century.

The spread of houses was not total and the area is fortunate today in retaining some large open spaces. Hornsey Wood in the south of the parish became the 120 acres of Finsbury Park. Highgate Woods were saved, by campaigning, from development and Crouch End playing fields provides 40 acres of adjacent open space. Coldfall Woods, at Fortis Green, survived until the 1920s and a remnant of this old woodland remains.

Four hundred acres of Tottenham Wood farm stretched to the north of Hornsey parish, much of it to become Alexandra Park, opened in 1863, and Muswell Hill Golf Course, opened in 1893. These provide a welcome green lung. In Alexandra Park the huge Alexandra Palace was opened in 1873 and its financial failures with 19th-century owners sometimes meant land was sold off from the Park to provide funds. But since 1901 the park has been preserved by Act of Parliament in local authority ownership.

Most of the photographs were taken in the heyday of the picture postcard, between 1902 and 1915, and the Edwardian scenes still have a rural feel. This is not only due to the horse transport but to the comparatively empty streets in which people stand without fear of fast moving traffic. Perhaps the motorised vehicle has done more to change the local way of life than the terraced street. As car ownership has spread so our way of life has changed. Now shopping is increasingly done by car, public transport has declined, streets have become lined with parked vehicles, making them less visually attractive and traffic lights, pedestrian crossings, railings and islands have altered our way of moving about our locality. The sadness is that the trend continues. But there are signs that people are waking up to the environmental cost and these photographs at least allow us to savour a different pace of life.

The photographs were taken by people with plate cameras who recorded the often new streets. Exposure times on occasions made it necessary for pedestrians to stand still and pose. The market seems to have been newly-moved-in inhabitants who purchased cards to send to their relatives and friends. By 1914, aided by new Post Office regulations, the number of cards sent that year had risen to 880m. After the First World War black and white cards seem to have dropped out of fashion.

In our own day we owe a debt to the patient collectors who assemble these reminders of the Edwardian scene. Hornsey Historical Society is fortunate in having Dick Whetstone among its members. Over the past decades he has assembled a unique collection relating to the Hornsey area. Dick Whetstone generously made his card collection available and the captions to them have been written by Hornsey Historical Society members Ian Murray, Joan Schwitzer, Malcolm Stokes and myself.

Ken Gay
August 1989

THE BOROUGH ARMS OF HORNSEY

The Borough Arms illustrated on a postcard published by Stoddart & Co. of Halifax in their 'Ja-Ja' heraldic series which covered almost every city and town in the British Isles.

Hornsey became a chartered borough in the County of Middlesex in 1903, having been previously administered as an urban district (1894), a local board of health (1867) and as a parish. The borough existed until 1965 when it joined with the boroughs of Wood Green and Tottenham to form the London Borough of Haringey. The coat of arms was granted in 1904, the oak trees denoting Hornsey's historic association with woodlands and the motto meaning 'Stronger by which more prepared'. The heraldic description is 'Per chevron argent and gules, in chief two oak trees eradicated proper and in base two swords in saltire proper, the latter pommelled and hilted or'.

FORTITOR QUO PARATIOR

HORNSEY.

1

HIGHGATE HIGH STREET, c.1885

Opened on 29th May, 1884, the cable tramway up and down Highgate Hill was the first in Europe. It ran between Highgate School at the top of the High Street to Highgate (Archway) station, the pulley mechanism being in premises further down the hill than the tram in the picture, on the left. The line was closed for several years after a tram broke loose, killing several people but was re-opened and ran till 1909, when it closed for electrification. The view looks south east along Highgate High Street, which itself has been preserved almost intact, though shops have changed trades as well as proprietors. The Angel public house on the right remains, along with many other Highgate hostelries, though its exterior has been remodelled.

HIGHGATE HIGH STREET, c.1935

The view is from South Grove. Highgate Pharmacy, established c.1800, can be seen on the extreme right, the proprietor then being H. E. Bailey. Next door at no. 66 (left) was Hinton's the draper's, and further along to the left, at no. 82, with wooden canopy (one of two still remaining today in the High Street) were J. B. Widden & Son, butchers. The general configuration remains the same today. The Gate House Inn, the half-timbered building to be seen at the end of the street and the old village graveyard opposite, have hardly altered at all.

SOUTHWOOD LANE, HIGHGATE, c.1905

The view is towards Archway Road. On the left is the entrance to the offices of the Hornsey Borough Council, built in 1869 and in use until Hornsey Town Hall was opened in Crouch End in 1934. Beyond the entrance are the secluded grounds of Park House, now the site of present day Hillcrest housing estate. On the extreme right is the wall of Southwood Lodge, home of J. G. Johnson, head of a firm of assayers to the Bank of England. In the middle, where Jacksons Lane forks to the right, is Bank Point, an eighteenth-century house which still remains. Out of sight behind it are some small shops but these have since been demolished.

4

HIGHGATE RAILWAY STATION, c.1910

Highgate station was originally opened in 1867 as part of the Edgware, Highgate and London Railway. The central platform replaced the side platforms in about 1883. This view looks north and on the left are the steep slopes below Archway Road. On the right a line of poplar trees were planted many years before on the edge of the grounds of The Priory, a big house built in the 1820s but demolished in c.1902 to make way for housing development on Shepherds Hill and for a new street named Priory Gardens. Beyond the station buildings, at the far end, is the footpath going up to Wood Lane. The view was published by the North London Picture Postcard Company of Finsbury Park.

THE MAIN AVENUE, HIGHGATE WOODS.

HIGHGATE WOOD, c.1906

Highgate Wood consists of 70 acres presented to the City of London by the Ecclesiastical Commissioners in 1886. The gift was preceded by a public campaign to prevent the woodland being sold for speculative building. In the Middle Ages the wood formed a small part of the Bishop of London's hunting forest. By Edwardian times, when this picture was taken, management of the wood was on the lines of a municipal park; note the 'rustic' fencing, designed to keep visitors to the prescribed path. The family taking a stroll is formally dressed, with mother and children wearing elaborate hats and father a bowler.

MUSWELL HILL ROAD, c.1907

Cranley Parade and Mansions, a tall Edwardian terrace, uncompromisingly urban in appearance, stands incongruously today against the background of Highgate Wood in a district of two- or at most three-storied suburban housing. Its *raison d'etre*, was Cranley Gardens railway station seen to the right of this picture, which opened in 1902, and continued in operation until 1957 but has since been demolished. The Parade was completed c.1904, with extensive housing development in prospect on the eastern flank (right) of Muswell Hill Road. Trades of the shops where the names are visible are: Thomas Crowther & Co., tobacconists; J. T. Wyman, a dairy; T. B. Lever, a painter and joiner; F. J. Harrison, a newsagent; Ainslie Brothers, butchers (and apparently the first shop in the Parade to open). Shops continue to be operated today but with different trades.

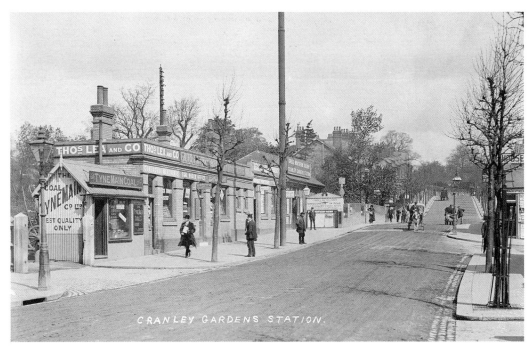

CRANLEY GARDENS STATION, c.1912

Opened in Muswell Hill on 2nd August 1902, Cranley Gardens was the intermediate station between Highgate and Muswell Hill on a branch of the 1863 Edgware, Highgate and London Railway. Constructed to serve Alexandra Palace, opened in May 1873, the branch was operated by the Great Northern Railway which owned the main EH and L Railway. Under London Transport ownership, pre-second World War plans for electrification were abandoned after the war. The line continued to operate as a steam railway but passenger services were withdrawn in July 1954 and in 1957 goods traffic ceased. The coal order office, seen in the picture, of Thomas Lea & Co., was one of many in North London; Thomas Lea himself lived in nearby Highgate. The station has been demolished.

FORTIS GREEN, c.1910

Fortis Green connects East Finchley with Muswell Hill. This leafy, narrow stretch remains with surviving, listed early 19th-century villas (left) and terraces of similar period on the right. Western Road (right) was, with Eastern and Southern Roads, laid out in the 1850s as Haswell Park Estate, now part of the Fortis Green conservation area. Building plots were taken up slowly over a long period of time. Further along towards Muswell Hill other 19th-century cottages survive, including some back-to-backs.

MUSWELL HILL POLICE STATION, 1911

The station was built in Fortis Green in 1904, on the site of a brewery. It was one of several new police stations opened in North London in the Edwardian era as the area became more heavily populated. It remains virtually unchanged today. This view shows it specially decorated for the coronation of King George V and Queen Mary, with the force grouped outside its main frontage.

FORTIS GREEN, c.1910

Looking towards the junction of Fortis Green with Tetherdown (left), Queens Avenue (ahead) and Fortis Green Road (right). On the right is Leaside Avenue, its name depicted on the gas street light to help the traveller at night. The white house is Fairport and the flats to the right of it The Gables, both locally listed as good examples of turn of the century Arts and Crafts architecture. On the extreme left can be seen the end of St. James's church school built on the site in 1850 and demolished in 1970.

11

MUSWELL HILL CONGREGATIONAL CHURCH, c.1910

Built on the corner of Tetherdown and Queens Avenue (right) in 1898-1901 on a site given by James Edmondson, the Highbury builder who developed Muswell Hill as an Edwardian suburb. The architect was 28-year-old Morley Horder. Following the merger in 1972 of the Congregationalists and the Presbyterians, the church is now the United Reformed Church. The palings and pillar-box have gone and the junction is now controlled by traffic lights. The trees (left) disappeared in 1921 when Woodside block of flats, built by Collins, replaced a mansion of the same name on the site. At that time Coldfall Wood reached to the boundary of the estate at the rear.

PAGES LANE, c.1906

Built at Muswell Hill in the 1860s, this small group of houses and cottages on the corner of Pages Lane (right) and Coppetts Road still survive today. Tetherdown, the road that leads up to them and continues as Coppetts Road was Tatterdown in the 19th century, until the local board changed the name, and this corner was once known as Tatterdown Place. The standpipe on the extreme left was used to replenish water carts that cleaned the roads, but it is a piece of street furniture which has now gone. Where the bearded man stands is now a traffic island. Coppetts Road leads north and now ends at the North Circular Road, built in 1929.

Grand Parade, Fortis Green Road, Muswell Hill. No. 1916.

FORTIS GREEN ROAD, c.1914

Grand parade on the left with its 1901 date stone to be seen in Queens Avenue (extreme left) stands today in Muswell Hill virtually unchanged, except for the shop fronts. In the distance can be seen St. James's church, completed with spire in 1910. The unbuilt site on the right was acquired by the church for a hall in 1911 but it was not built until 1925 when a war memorial building was erected to the designs of architect George Grey Wornum, the architect who later built the headquarters of the Royal Institute of British Architects in Portland Place.

Fortis Green Road, Muswell Hill   London

7. 15. 03

Stengel & Co., London E. C. 39 Redcross Street 19684

FORTIS GREEN ROAD, c.1903

The arched windows of St. James's Parade, built by Edmondson in 1901, at the southern end of Fortis Green Road, still survive, but many are now covered by often unattractive fascia boards. The canvas awnings have disappeared, as has the Athenaeum (right). The kerb is now usually lined with cars. Most of the upper two storeys are used as residential flats.

THE ATHENAEUM, c.1905

The Athenaeum concert hall was built in 1901 by James Edmondson next to his St. James's Parade in Fortis Green Road, Muswell Hill. It was the venue for many local activities and in its time it housed clubs, choirs, amateur dramatics, dancing, cinemas, schools and a synagogue. Meetings of Muswell Hill Parliament, a form of debating society based on the House of Commons, were held here for many years. It was acquired in the early 1960s by J. Sainsbury as a site for a supermarket and demolished. On the corner opposite (left) an Odeon cinema and complex of shops and flats were built in 1936.

19 — LONDON. - MUSWELL-HILL.

GRAND AVENUE, c.1905

The view is taken in Muswell Hill Road looking towards Princes Parade in Muswell Hill Broadway. Grand Avenue, on the left, was built by William J. Collins from 1900 as one of several avenues on his Fortismere Estate between Muswell Hill Road and Fortis Green. No. 1, seen here, is virtually unchanged today. The tree has gone, though a few, late-19th-century, well-built, terraced houses still stand here. On the right is part of the newly rebuilt St. James's church, as yet without its tower and spire, completed in 1910.

ST. JAMES'S CHURCH, c.1911

Completed in 1910, with tower and spire rising to a height of 179ft at one of the highest spots in Muswell Hill, St. James's is a notable landmark. The building of a new church to replace an earlier 19th-century church was begun in 1899 as the new suburb was being developed. Bombed during the Second World War it was restored in 1952 and currently has a sizeable congregation. The view is from the top end of St. James's Lane which is virtually unchanged today, except for the intrusion of parked vehicles.

St. James Lane, Muswell Hill, N.

ST. JAMES'S LANE, c.1908

Sheltered St. James's Lane, which curves down from St. James's church to join Muswell Hill was the location for villas and cottages during the 19th century before the Edwardian suburb was developed. By 1873 a viaduct was built across it to take the branch railway to Alexandra Palace, close to a tiny, weatherboarded public house called The Royal Oak. This view is taken near the lowest point of St. James's Lane, looking up towards the Hill. The building of the railway line, with a station at Muswell Hill, led to some late 19th-century housing being built in this area.

QUEENS PARADE, c.1930

Queens Parade (left) erected in 1897, was the first of the shopping parades built by James Edmondson when he created the new suburb of Muswell Hill. Each parade was given a separate name but since the 1960s the parades have all been numbered as Muswell Hill Broadway. W. H. Smith still occupy the shop on the left where they have been since 1912. In the distance can be seen the roundabout and the spire of Muswell Hill Baptist Church. The turning on the right is Summerland Gardens.

DAIRY SHOP, MUSWELL HILL, c.1905

This shop in Queens Parade, on the corner with Queens Avenue, opened in 1897, with Manor Farm Dairy as its first occupants. Delivery of milk was by churns on handcarts until replaced by the milk bottle. In the 1930s Manor Farm Dairy became part of United Dairies. In recent years the shop has changed into a general food store, but the building is still recognisable today.

With Heartiest Christmas Greetings and Best Wishes
for the New Year from . . .

𝔐𝔯. 𝔞𝔫𝔡 𝔐𝔯𝔰. 𝔍. 𝔚. 𝔉𝔩𝔢𝔱𝔠𝔥𝔢𝔯 𝔉𝔬𝔯𝔡
. . 𝔞𝔫𝔡 𝔉𝔞𝔪𝔦𝔩𝔶. . .

5, QUEENS AVENUE,
MUSWELL HILL,
LONDON, N.

PERSONALISED CHRISTMAS CARD, 1904

Mr and Mrs J. W. Fletcher Ford and family, of 5 Queens Avenue, Muswell Hill, posted this personalised greetings card in December 1904. Queens Avenue had been built in 1898 by James Edmondson as the most prestigious road in the new suburb. Today many of its very large houses have been converted into hotels, or divided into flats.

MUSWELL HILL, 1890

Looking towards the top of the Hill and the Green man, seen on the right. This junction was once known as the Plantation, occupying a site where there once had been a village pond. When the suburb was built, at the end of the 19th century, Queens Avenue and Dukes Avenue were added to the meeting place of Muswell Hill Road (now Broadway), Muswell Hill and Colney Hatch Lane, making a five road junction. It is now a traffic roundabout, with a public toilet building and a diesel bus terminus at its centre. There are no trees left on the site.

HORSE BUSES AT MUSWELL HILL, c.1905

On 28th April 1901, a service of twelve, three-horse omnibuses commenced running between Charing Cross and Muswell Hill, each making five journeys a day. There were other buses, making 24 journeys in all, some proceeding along Colney Hatch Lane. The view is of the roundabout area at Muswell Hill where, in 1902, the council authorised the building of a stand for the horse buses. The clock above Sainsbury's was installed in 1903. In 1912 the horse buses were replaced by petrol buses.

The Exchange, Muswell Hill London

Stengel & Co., London E. C. 39 Redcross Street 19683

THE EXCHANGE, 1903

The Exchange shopping parades were built at the Muswell Hill roundabout site by James Edmondson from 1900. This developer also laid out Dukes Avenue and gave the site for the Baptist church (centre). The horse trough of 1902 has been preserved and moved to nearby Queens Avenue. Sainsbury's remained here until the mid 1960s when their supermarket opened in Fortis Green Road on the site of the Athenaeum hall.

Green Man, Muswell Hill.

THE GREEN MAN, c.1910

The Green Man has stood on this site at the top of Muswell Hill at least from the early 19th century, but probably for much longer, as an ale house is recorded for Muswell Hill in 1552. The inn would have served travellers on the medieval road to the north, along Colney Hatch Lane. In this view the horse stands outside the old, stone built building. Beyond it is the taller late 19th-century addition, built as an hotel extension. In recent years the whole building has been altered and refaced but it continues to operate as a public house. The building left of the stone portion, probably dating from the eighteenth century, also survives, now in use as a restaurant. Next to it (extreme left) is an Edwardian shopping parade.

S 6437   MUSWELL HILL STATION G N R'LY.

MUSWELL HILL RAILWAY STATION c.1910

Opened in 1873 and situated on Muswell Hill, just below The Green Man, the station was on the Great Northern Railway branch line from Highgate to Alexandra Palace. By 1910 the station was served by 61 trains a day for travel to Kings Cross and the City of London. Passenger services by steam train continued until July 1954 and goods services until 1956. Pre-Second World War plans for electrification, so that the line would become part of the system operated by London Transport, were abandoned in 1952, despite a good deal of the work having already been completed. The site is now occupied by Muswell Hill Junior and Infants School and the line of the railway is used as the Parkland Walk.

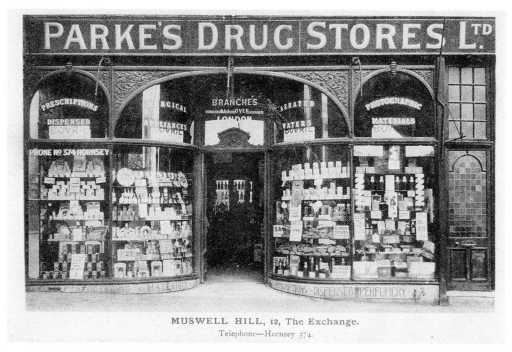

MUSWELL HILL, 12, The Exchange.
Telephone—Hornsey 374.

PARKE'S DRUG STORES, c.1908

In September 1901, Parke's Drug Stores announced the opening of another store 'on their usual magnificent scale' at no. 12 The Exchange, Muswell Hill, the parade of shops newly built by James Edmondson. The shop front style is typical for its date. Today the store is occupied by Boots the Chemists, with modern shop front.

MUSWELL HILL BROADWAY, c.1937

Looking from the roundabout towards Colney Hatch Lane. The building on the left was built in 1898 as a branch of the London and Provincial Bank. By 1924 it had become a branch of Barclays Bank, which it remains today. The shopping parade to the right of it was known as Station Parade. Centre is a Belisha Beacon, named after Leslie Hore-Belisha, Minister of Transport who introduced them in the 1930s along with other measures to make roads safer. On the right, Parkes' remains at no. 12, The Exchange but with a more modern shop name fascia, calling itself chemists rather than drug stores.

COLNEY HATCH LANE, c.1910

Looking north from Muswell Hill Broadway, with the Wesleyan Methodist Church on the corner of Alexandra Park Road on the right. First developed in the 1880s, modern design bicycles became widely popular in the Edwardian period and must have helped women in their struggle for equality of opportunity.

WESLEYAN METHODIST CHURCH, c.1930

The Muswell Hill Wesleyan Methodist Church, built on the corner of Colney Hatch Lane and Alexandra Park Road, was opened in April, 1899. The adjacent church hall, on the right, was opened in October 1904. Both were demolished in 1984 and replaced by blocks of flats. A new church was opened by the Methodists on their North Bank property in nearby Pages Lane.

31

COLNEY HATCH LANE, c.1905

Looking towards Muswell Hill Broadway, with the sign on the left pointing towards Pages Lane. Colney Hatch Lane is part of an early medieval route between London and the north, via Whetstone and Barnet. Further along towards Muswell Hill on the east side (left) in medieval times, was the spring and chapel visited by pilgrims. Muswell Hill derives its name from this spring, reputed to have effected a miraculous cure on a Scottish king. The well has been built over and is no longer to be seen, although it survived until the end of the 19th century.

MUSWELL HILL FARMHOUSE, 1917

Dating from 1670, this farmhouse stood in Coppetts Road, north of Muswell Hill. It survived until the 1930s, with Wilton Road built alongside it on the south, and Sutton Road on the north. Another farmhouse also survived to the north east of it in Colney Hatch Lane. These were in the parish of Friern Barnet which remained comparatively rural till after 1919 when remaining farmlands began to be built over.

ISOLATION HOSPITAL, c.1908

Coppetts Wood hospital originated in 1888 as an isolation hospital for Hornsey. It was built in Coppetts Road on former waste land, near the boundary with Friern Barnet. Additions and reconstructions have been made over the years but the building in Coppetts Road is still recognisable today. In 1988 the hospital became an integral part of the Royal Free. It has 109 beds, 87 for infectious diseases.

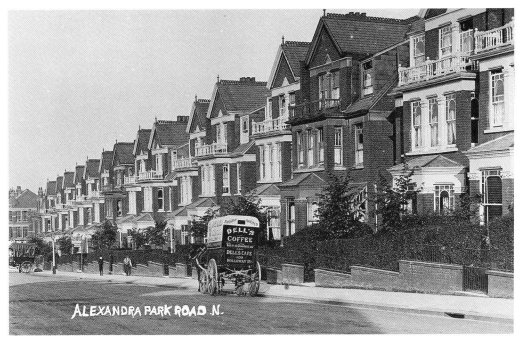

ALEXANDRA PARK ROAD, c.1910

This long road runs today from Colney Hatch Lane, Muswell Hill to Alexandra Palace railway station in Wood Green. It is shewn as laid out but not yet built up on the 1894 Ordnance Survey map. Development occurred from the turn of the century, including the 1907 parade of shops at the extreme left of this view. Also built in the long road were three churches: St. Andrews (1903), St. Saviours (1904) and Whitefield Memorial Congregational (1907). The days of coffee and other grocery deliveries by horse and cart have long gone, but the view otherwise is much the same today.

SHOPS IN ALEXANDRA PARK ROAD, c.1910

The date 1907 is still to be seen above the corner shop, which is at the junction of Alexandra Park Road and Rosebery Road. The shop fascias have changed, and the parade has lost its pristine Edwardian appearance, but all the shops are in use and continue to serve the surrounding residential area. During the 1930s, when inter-war building filled vacant housing plots, (aided by the extension of the Piccadilly line to Bounds Green), this parade was extended (left, beyond picture) to the corner of The Avenue. Above the shops are residential flats.

ALEXANDRA PALACE AND PARK, c.1880

Alexandra Park was first opened in 1863 on former farmlands lying between Muswell Hill and Wood Green. Using building materials from the demolished 1862 South Kensington exhibition building, the palace was slowly built, and opened in 1873. It was burnt down sixteen days later and this second palace building, designed by John Johnston, was opened in 1875. This early photograph shows the scene before landscaping round the palace was completed. The building was attacked by another fire in July 1980 but it has subsequently been rebuilt and reopened in 1988.

ALEXANDRA PALACE, c.1905

The view of the north-east corner of the building, seen from across the boating lake. The palace is built on a site some 300 feet above sea level and can be seen widely from the surrounding flatter lands of the Lee and Thames valleys. It covers nearly eight acres. The lake was due to be built over for housing in 1900 but was saved at the last moment from development by the consortium of local authorities which purchased the palace and park in February 1901.

THE GREAT HALL, c.1905

The Great Hall was the main feature of Alexandra Palace. Measuring 386 feet in length and 184 feet in width, it could seat 12,000 people. Statues of kings and queens of England stood along the base of the colonnades. The hall, with its rows of supporting columns, was destroyed by the 1980 fire, which started near the organ. It has been replaced by a new hall of the same size which has a self-supporting roof, so that the columns have been dispensed with.

FLOWER SHOW AND WILLIS ORGAN, c.1905

Flower shows were among the events held in the Great Hall at Alexandra Palace. In this view can be seen the huge, eight thousand pipe organ built by 'Father' Henry Willis in 1873-74. It was restored in 1929-30 when it was converted from steam to electric action, but suffered during the Second World War from the effects of a flying bomb which fell in The Avenue (behind it) and damaged the roof above it. The organ had to be dismantled and stored and was nearly sold. Rebuilding after the 1980 fire includes the restoration of the organ by Henry Willis IV, great grandson of the builder, to be completed once sufficient funds are raised.

CONSERVATORY, c.1907

The Great Hall of Alexandra Palace was flanked on both its east and west sides by courts, and beyond them, by glass roofed conservatories. The west conservatory is know as the Palm Court. Restoration of the glass domed roofs has been undertaken as part of the reconstruction after the 1980 fire.

BANDSTAND, c.1907

Band concerts were a popular feature at Alexandra Palace and this bandstand was included among its facilities.

ITALIAN GARDENS, c.1920

The court between the Great Hall of Alexandra Palace and the western conservatory was known as the Italian Gardens. The fountain was one of its main features. After the 1980 fire the site was used for another exhibition hall and the fountain was moved to the rose garden in the park, on the east side of the palace.

ZOOLOGICAL COLLECTION, c.1905

Three thousand people paid 1*d* on August Bank Holiday, 1905 to see the zoological collection. Consisting mainly of birds and small animals donated to the Trustees by the public over the years, it included small kangaroos, a mongoose and paradoc cats.

ALEXANDRA PALACE, Monkey House and Zoological Collection.

Animals, etc., under the control of Captain HENRY, late of Jno. & Geo. Sanger. *Secretary & Manager* — EDWIN GOODSHIP.

MONKEY HOUSE AND ZOO, c.1907

A monkey house was a popular feature at Alexandra Palace. The zoological collection included many birds, with a lofty aviary in the Palm Court. Edwin Goodship (name bottom right) retired as secretary and manager of Alexandra Palace in 1909.

Animals, etc., under the control of Capt. HENRY, late of Jno. & Geo. Sanger.
Secretary and Manager—EDWIN GOODSHIP.

**MONKEY HOUSE AND ZOOLOGICAL
COLLECTION, c.1907**

The monkey house had been at the Alexandra Palace at least since the 1880s. A small room off the Palm Court was used for them. The picture shows that stuffed animals were also featured among the display cases.

'NELSON', THE TEDDY BEAR, c.1905

The famous teddy bear, 'Nelson', still remembered from their childhood by older local residents, was very popular.

The Famous Teddy Bear, "NELSON."
Presented by Messrs. THOMAS WALLIS & CO., Holborn Circus.

ALEXANDRA PARK, 1912

In addition to the leisure facilities within Alexandra Palace, which included roller-skating, bowls, boxing and other sports as well as concerts, opera, pantomine and cinema shows, there were a range of events held in the grounds. These included the circus, firework displays, rallies, kite flying, competitive parachuting from balloons, and fairground entertainments, of which this switchback seems to be an example.

AIRSHIP, c.1905

The pioneering airship was constructed in a shed in Alexandra Park from 1903 by Dr Barton. Its only flight was in 1905 when it was wrecked on landing in Essex. The site of the shed was later adapted as a football field, adjacent to the boating lake, leased from 1935 by the Alexandra Park Football Club (founded 1889). The entrance to the park from Bedford Road, Wood Green is shewn. This remained substantially unaltered till the 1980s, although from 1905 it was on the tram route to the Palace from Wood Green, converted in 1938 into a bus route passing through Alexandra Park.

BAND OF HOPE FESTIVAL, ALEXANDRA PALACE, MAY 1908.
TABLEAU. NURSES AND GIPSIES. 3RD AWARD.

BAND OF HOPE FESTIVAL, 1908

Rallies in the palace and park were held by church, political and educational associations, especially in the summer months. This shows a tableau of nurses and gypsies staged at the Band of Hope festival of May 1908.

169. The Grove, Alexandra Palace.

THE GROVE, c.1906

The Grove takes its name from the ancient estate on the north side of Muswell Hill, below the Green Man, which was added to Alexandra Park when it opened in 1863. The house itself was demolished when the 1873 railway line to Alexandra Palace was built. The Grove remains a pleasant area within Alexandra Park where concerts have always been popular. The bandstand has been removed but concerts are still held.

BELGIAN REFUGEES, 1914

By September 1914 Alexandra Palace had been taken over for the housing of Belgian refugees after the invasion of their country by the Germans at the start of the First World War. The Great Hall was used for sleeping and feeding. By adapting the skating rink and other palace spaces, some three thousand could be housed at one time. By March 1915, when the Belgian occupation of the palace was ended, some 38,000 had passed through.

HERZLICHE
WEIHNACHTS und NEUJAHRS
1916 GRÜSSE 1917
aus der
KRIEGSGEFANGENSCHAFT im
Alexandra Palace
LONDON N.
Sign: W. Holt
BATT: E.   P.o.W. No. 3711
COMP.: 4   CORP.: 2

INTERNMENT CAMP, c.1916

After the Belgian refugees left in 1915 Alexandra Palace and Park became an internment camp, where up to three thousand enemy aliens could be held. In 1916 the 2,334 prisoners included 1,598 German and 695 Austrian soldiers. This Christmas and New Year card was sent in 1916 by W. Holst, P.O.W. no. 3711.

PALACE PARADE, PRIORY ROAD, c.1912

The exit from Alexandra Park on the Hornsey side leads out to the foot of Muswell Hill and to Park Road and Priory Road. The Palace Parade of shops was built in 1906 on the corner of Park and Priory Roads, opposite the exit to the park. The site had been previously occupied by weather-boarded Rose Villa, pulled down in 1902. The building of this corner meant the loss of the last farmlands in the area. Trams began to run along Priory Road in 1905 with a service extending up to the palace. Trams were later replaced by diesel buses. The central island shewn in the view has gone and the junction is controlled by traffic lights. The shops remain.

REDSTON ROAD, c.1910

Redston Road is the most westerly of the six substantial terraces laid out north from Priory road in the Edwardian period. The lands were owned by the Warner family as the Priory Estate, stretching back to what had become the grounds of Alexandra Park. The estate was the site of an 1820s Gothic revival style mansion called The Priory which was demolished in 1902. In this view the huge bulk of Alexandra Palace can be seem looming in the background. The scene is substantially unchanged today.

PRIORY ROAD, c.1908

In March 1899 plans submitted by architect John Farrer 'for laying out the frontage of the Priory Estate to the north of Priory Road and for private carriage drives running parallel to Priory Road' were approved by Hornsey Urban District Council. By June 1901 villa residences were being advertised at £65 per year rental. The Moravian Church (left) was consecrated in 1908 and is still in use.

ST. GEORGE'S CHURCH, c.1910

On the south side of Priory Road, on the corner with Park Avenue South, St. George's church was built in 1907 to the designs of architect J. S. Alder, to serve the new residential area being developed each side of Priory Road. Extended in 1928 it was bombed in 1940 and demolished in 1956. The replacement church of St. George's was built on a new site on the corner of Park Road and Cranley Gardens and consecrated in 1959. It has subsequently absorbed the congregation of the demolished Hornsey parish church of St. Mary's and is known as St. Mary's with St. George. This Priory Road site is now occupied by Hornsey fire staiton built in 1963 to replace fire stations in Tottenham Lane, Hornsey and Fortis Green, Muswell Hill.

PLEASURE GROUNDS, c.1910

Some eight acres of low lying land between Priory Road and Middle Lane, Hornsey, were laid out in 1894 as Pleasure Grounds by Hornsey Urban District Council. The drinking fountain, (centre rear) was moved to this site in 1895 from Crouch End Broadway. In 1926 the pleasure grounds were extended by the purchase of Lewcock's field, fronting Priory Road, and the whole renamed Priory Park.

PRIORY GARDENS, c.1905

The views are all taken in the public pleasure grounds acquired in the 1890s and named after the house and park which was situated on the north side of Priory Road called The Priory. The photographer uses the same location twice, which suggests he was more interested in marketing the postcard to the individuals posed in the photograph. The round flower bed later accommodated the fifty-ton fountain from St. Paul's cathedral churchyard, unveiled at Hornsey in 1909, and still *in situ* in Priory Park today.

59

Priory Road, Hornsey. N.

PRIORY ROAD, c.1910

Plans for the parade of seven shops on the left were approved in April 1899 by Hornsey Urban District Council. They still stand, substantially unchanged, terminating at the corner of Nightingale Lane. Tramcars began to run along Priory Road from Wood Green in 1905, journeying either to the foot of Muswell Hill or up to Alexandra Palace. They were replaced in 1938 by buses, with the tram route to the Palace replaced by a road to Wood Green through the park.

MIDDLE LANE, HORNSEY, c.1903

The view looks north towards Priory Road, with the pleasure grounds, opened in 1894, on the left. The Wesleyan Methodist church on the right was opened in 1886 and seated 1,000 people. It was demolished in 1975 and replaced by a smaller church. Note the street trees, newly planted by the council.

PARK ROAD, c.1905

Leading from Crouch End Broadway towards Alexandra Park, from which it derives its name, this road is an ancient route. From the 16th to the 19th century it was called Maynard Street after Stephen Maynard who had become Lord of Topsfield Manor at Crouch End. The Maynard Arms, the tall building on the left, standing on the corner of Lynton Road, dates from 1851 and perpetuates the former name. Park Terrace (left) has gone. Park Villas behind the vegetation on the right survived from the mid-19th century until 1977 when the terrace was replaced by new housing.

PLAYING FIELDS, CROUCH END.

CROUCH END PLAYING FIELDS, c.1905

Situated west of Park Road, Crouch End, these fields are a remnant of a farm ploughed by oxen in the 14th century to provide food for the table of the lord of Hornsey manor, the Bishop of London. By the 16th century it was known as Rowledge Farm and the arable was being turned to grass. The farm extended from Park Road to Crouch End Hill and Hornsey Lane. There were sheep until the 1880s, giving Shepherds Hill its name. Dairy cows followed until 1892 when the Ecclesiastical Commissioners leased out the land, which has been used since by a number of sports clubs.

Bp. of Willesden.
Dr. Perrin

THE HORNSEY WAR MEMORIAL, 1921

The Borough of Hornsey's war memorial took the form of an extension to the Cottage Hospital in Park Road, later known as Hornsey Central Hospital. The Bishop of Willesden, Dr Perrin, is shown with senior Army officers taking part in the dedication ceremony, held on Armistice Day, 11th November 1921 in the presence of a huge crowd.

HORNSEY CARNIVAL, 1907

The Carnival was in aid of the Hornsey Cottage Hospital Fund. The procession formed at Cranley Gardens at 5 p.m. on 26th September, 1907 and was three-quarters-of-a-mile long. It followed a circuitous route through Highgate and Turnpike Lane, arriving back at Crouch End at 9.30 p.m., after dark. The float in this picture anticipates the laying of the Hospital foundation stone in 1910. One of the drivers in this picture received first prize for decorating his house in Gisburn Road on the route of the procession with 850 lights.

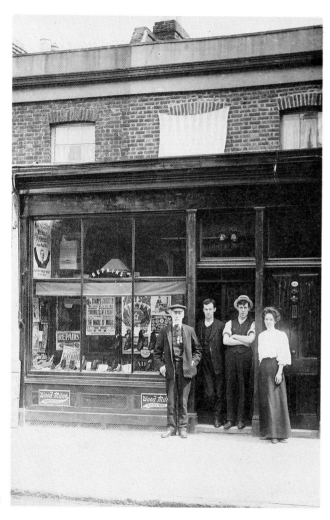

SHOP AT 116 PARK ROAD, c.1905

This shop in Park Road, Crouch End, had long been a shoemaker's, where boots and shoes could be made to measure, as well as mended. The photograph was probably taken around 1905 when Walter F. Sears seems to have taken over the shop from Arthur Horgan. It was still Sears & Son in 1938. The premises were part of a terrace of shops and houses between the Maynard Arms and Palace Road that was bombed during the Second World War and has since been redeveloped.

Crouch End School Cricket Team 1912 Season
Middx

CROUCH END SCHOOL CRICKET TEAM, 1912

Crouch End school in Wolsley Road, off Park Road, was built in 1877 as the first of Hornsey's Board schools. The much altered building was extensively damaged by fire in 1989 but the notable woodwork building of 1893 on the corner of Park Road survives. The school is now known as Highgate Wood. In the picture the board on the ground records the results of the 1912 season. The inevitable question is, how did these boys fare during the 1914-18 war?

CROUCH END HIGH SCHOOL AND COLLEGE N8

PUPILS OF CROUCH END HIGH SCHOOL, c.1918

Crouch End High School and College, a private girl's school based at Elm House in Middle Lane, achieved fame under its founder and head, Miss Charlotte Cowdroy, for her insistence on 'womanliness' alongside academic attainments. In 1937 the school moved to larger premises in Hornsey Lane. This photograph appears to depict the pupils in 1918 victory celebrations.

CROUCH END CLOCKTOWER, 1895

The picture shows the unveiling ceremony on 22nd June, 1895. The clocktower was built in his lifetime to honour H. R. Williams (1822-97), wine merchant and leading local Liberal politician whose successful campaigns included saving Highgate Woods from development. The clocktower still stands today as the focal point of the district.

TOPSFIELD PARADE, c.1925

Topsfield Parade of shops was built in Crouch End in 1895 between Middle Lane and Tottenham Lane. It was put up by James Edmondson of Highbury on the site of ancient Topsfield Manor and its grounds. An 1895 date stone can be seen at the junction of Tottenham Lane and Elder Avenue. This 1920s photograph shows Marks and Spencer's, long gone from the scene. Traffic lights now operate at this junction.

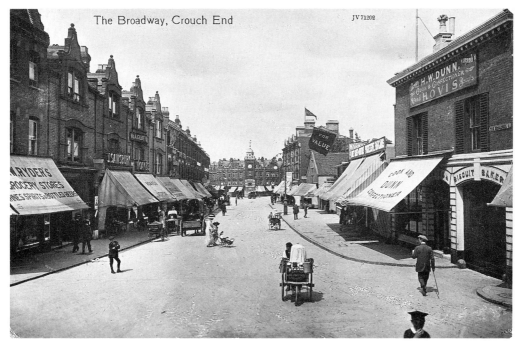

CROUCH END BROADWAY, c.1910

Looking towards the 1895 clocktower from the foot of Crouch Hill. Dunn's bakery (right), surmounted by stone wheatsheaf and 1850 datestone, survived the urbanisation of the village centre in the 1880s and 1890s and is still the scene of a thriving business. Lake House Villa, at right angles to the road beyond Dunn's, became the site in 1934 of the electricity showrooms adjacent to Hornsey town hall. Ryder's (left) survived until 1924 and Sainsbury's stayed on the site until the 1970s.

No. 179.   OLD SMITHY, CROUCH END IN 1890.

CROUCH END SMITHY, 1890

The old smithy stood near the centre of Crouch End village, at the junction of Crouch Hill and Crouch End Hill. It was removed in 1895, following the sale of the Topsfield estate lands, and replaced by a bank. A later bank building now stands on the site.

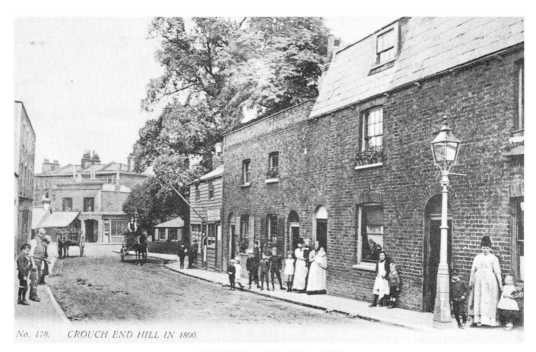

No. 178.   CROUCH END HILL IN 1890.

CROUCH END HILL, 1890

The view looks down Crouch End hill towards Crouch End Broadway, with the bakery to be seen in the distance (left) and the old smithy at the foot of the hill. Although Crouch End was urbanised in the 1880s and 1890s, some old buildings, such as these, survived until the 1920s and 1930s.

CROUCH HILL, c.1925

Harringay Arms remains in the late 19th-century parade of shops on the left and the road retains its narrow width. The junction of Crouch Hill with Crouch End Broadway (centre) is now controlled by traffic lights. In the distance can be seen the white shop front of J. Lyons & Company which had taken over no. 1 Crouch End Broadway by 1924. To the right J. Sainsbury's were at no. 5 by 1911 and Salmon & Son at no. 7 by 1920. All these shops have now gone from the scene.

CROUCH HILL, c.1915

The view is down Crouch Hill towards Crouch End Broadway. On the skyline is Alexandra Palace, not yet sporting the television mast (added in 1936). The single decker bus service to Finsbury Park station began in July 1914.

COOLHURST ROAD CROUCH END

COOLHURST ROAD, c.1910

Coolhurst Road, connecting Shepherds Hill with Crouch End, was laid out in 1882 on former Rowledge farmlands for C. S. Dickens by his agents, The Imperial Property Investment Company. East of it, twelve roads with 588 houses were laid out, many of them detached properties. Since 1945 some of them have been replaced by flats. The view looks north towards Shepherds Hill.

AVENUE ROAD, CROUCH END.

AVENUE ROAD, c.1910

Avenue Road, connecting Crescent Road, Crouch End with Stanhope Road (which leads into Shepherds Hill), was developed in the 1890s with large, good quality houses. Many have been replaced by post war apartment blocks.

CROUCH END HILL.

CROUCH END HILL, c.1905

Crouch End Hill is part of an ancient route from London which crosses a ridge known locally as the Hog's Back; the area came to be called Mount Pleasant. In 1863 Christchurch was built on Crouch End Hill on land given by C. S. Dickens. In the 1880s a private art school was built opposite it which was to become Hornsey College of Art. Large houses were built in the area.

Crouch End Station N.
from Hornsey Lane.

CROUCH END STATION, c.1910

Crouch End railway station was opened on Crouch End Hill, near the junction with Hornsey Lane in 1867. It was on the new Edgware, Highgate and London line from the City which opened up Crouch End and Highgate as commuter suburbs. The houses in Crescent Road, opposite the station, date from this period but most of Crouch End was built up about 20 years later as building land became available. The station buildings still survive but the line has been converted into the Parkland Walk, providing a green track between Finsbury Park and Muswell Hill.

HORNSEY RISE, 1907

These shops were at the northern end of Hornsey Road, which becomes Hornsey Rise leading into Crouch End Hill. At no. 501 was Thomas Laughlin, dealing with china and glass; it is now a dry cleaners. At no. 503 was Nash's Registry Office, where jobs were advertised and which doubled as a stationer's; it is now a newsagent. At no. 505 was a dairy, Emerton & Sons, later taken over by the United Dairies; it is now a food and general store. At no. 507 was Home & Colonial Tea Stores; the shop was recently a dress manufacturer but is now vacant. At no. 509 was Jackson Bros., cheesemongers; it is now a restaurant. At nos. 511 and 513 were Sanders Bros. corn merchants; it is now Londis, on the coner of Hazeville Road.

HORNSEY LANE, c.1910

The view shows Hornsey Lane at its junction with Sunnyside Road. Close inspection reveals a boundary plate which is still in place today at the foot of the corner pillar. Hornsey Lane follows a ridge which has been the boundary between Islington and Hornsey parishes from time immemorial. The road itself is much older than the boundary and probably a prehistoric ridgeway. In the mid-19th century there were views of open pasture and woodland on both sides of Hornsey Lane. Sunnyside Road was opened in the 1860s and named after the house in Hornsey Lane.

Stroud Green Station   Stapleton Hall Road   N.

STAPLETON HALL ROAD c.1910

The view is under the railway bridge in Stapleton Hall Road looking towards Stroud Green Road. Here the Edgware, Highgate and London line crossed the Tottenham and Hampstead Junction Railway. Stroud Green station was opened in 1881 on the E. H. & L. line to serve a rapidly growing urban area. Services ceased in the 1950s and the line has become the Parkland Walk with the stationmaster's house surviving as a community centre. The bridge remains.

74. Lancaster Road, Stroud Green N. and at Bowes Park.

LANCASTER ROAD, c.1912

The houses in Lancaster Road, off Stapleton Hall Road, were built in the early 1880s, following the opening of Stroud Green Station. No. 74, shewn here is at the northern end, near the railway and originally occupied by Edward Houghton & Son, builders, responsible for much local development. By 1911 the premises were occupied by Alfred Pryke whose building work apparently extended to Bowes Park, as this postcard, which served as a trade advertisement, shows. The house still remains today.

1322 Stroud Green.

CROUCH HILL, STROUD GREEN, c.1910

The view is up Crouch Hill from the top of Stroud Green Road, with Stapleton Hall Road on the right and Hanley Road on the left. The Stapleton public house (right) has been recently redecorated. Stopped outside is a horse bus, soon to be replaced by the petrol buses of the London General Omnibus Company. On the opposite corner (left) lies Friern Manor Dairy whose farm was near the present day junction of Colney Hatch Lane and the North Circular Road. Still surviving *in situ* on the Crouch Hill side of the dairy building are terracotta murals illustrating dairying in the past and as practised in the (then) modern way at Friern Manor at the turn of the century.

STROUD GREEN ROAD, c.1910

Before it began to be built up with shops and houses in the 1870s, Stroud Green Road was a narrow lane, marking part of the boundary between Hornsey on the east and Islington on the west. Apparently water-logged in wet weather, it well deserved its name Stroud, originally meaning a marshy place overgrown with bushes. Its development was held back in the 19th century through the reluctance of Charles Turner of Stapleton Hall, who farmed the land, to sell. The surrounding area was developed in the 1880s and Stroud Green Road soon became a busy shopping street. It has changed very little in the past century.

Stroud Green Road. N.

STROUD GREEN ROAD, c.1910

Little traffic is shewn in this view of Stroud Green Road which was to develop not only as a busy shopping centre but as a route into Seven Sisters Road and to Finsbury Park railway station. The station was opened as a halt called Seven Sisters at the point where the Great Northern Railway (opened in 1850) bridged both Seven Sisters and Stroud Green Roads. The station was renamed Finsbury Park when the nearby park was opened in 1869.

STROUD GREEN ROAD, c.1910

Horse transport and gas street lamps characterise this scene which looks towards the Stapleton public house. The shopping parades still remain today.

STROUD GREEN ROAD, c.1914

The solid tyred, single-decker bus shewn here, on the west side of Stroud Green Road, was on the petrol bus service between Finsbury Park and Muswell Hill started in 1914 by the London General Omnibus Company. Its introduction severely reduced passenger use of the steam train service between the two places. At Finsbury Park travellers could commute into the City and West End using Northern and Piccadilly line services which terminated there. The bus service continues to Muswell Hill today as the W7 double-decker diesel bus.

DRYLANDS ROAD, c.1905

Looking north towards the Baptist chapel, on the corner with Weston Park, Crouch End. This domed building replaced the first chapel, opened in 1889 on the adjacent site on the corner of Ferme Park Road. Built in 1900 to seat 1,250 persons, the second chapel accommodated regular congregations of over 1,000 in 1903. With the enormous drop in church attendance since that time, especially since the Second World War, the chapel was demolished in 1974, despite opposition from local conservationists. A new, smaller chapel has been erected on the site of the original place of worship.

RATHCOOLE GARDENS, c.1908

Rathcoole house and estate was developed by local builder, J. C. Hill on land stretching from Tottenham Lane back to Ridge Road. On the site Rathcoole Avenue, Rathcoole Gardens, Harvey Road and Uplands Road were laid out and some 257 terraced houses planned, though few had been built by 1896.

NELSON ROAD, c.1908

Terraced housing spread over the land between Stroud Green Road and Hornsey in the 1880s. Ferme Park Road had been laid out by 1880 and roads parallel with it by 1884. One of these was Nelson Road, originally named Oakworth Road, but renamed Nelson Road before 1900.

INDERWICK ROAD, c.1908

Inderwick Road runs parallel with Ferme Park and Nelson Roads and, like them, connects Ridge Road with Tottenham Lane. Building plots were for sale by 1888 on its Ferme Park Estate by the Streatham and Imperial Estate Company and Inderwick Road was built up in the 1890s.

TOTTENHAM LANE, c.1905

Topsfield Parade, Crouch End is on the extreme left, at the junction with Rosebery Gardens. Beyond it are houses on the site of the present Y.M.C.A. building. Holy Innocents' Church can be seen in the distance. On the right is Broadway Parade and beyond it is the garden of Lightcliffe House, demolished by 1910 to make way for a cinema, where the offices of the local newspaper, the *Hornsey Journal*, now stand. William Phillips's shop on the extreme right was a bootmaker, established c.1904.

HORNSEY. OLD AND NEW.

TOTTENHAM LANE, c.1935

The old and the new referred to here are Manor Cottages in Tottenham Lane, a group of seventeenth-century buildings which were demolished in 1935, and the Y.M.C.A. building, opened the previous year on the site between Rosebery Gardens and Elmfield Avenue. When the photograph was taken the Y.M.C.A. had just been built and the cottages were about to be demolished. The site of the latter is now occupied by a petrol station.

HOLY INNOCENTS' SCHOOL, c.1900

Erected in 1848 in Tottenham Lane, and the oldest purpose-built school building in the area, it was designed by a London architect, John Henry Taylor, for the parish of St. Mary's Hornsey, as the Hornsey National Infants' School. It provided schooling for about 100 children, changing its name to Holy Innocents' after it entered into association with new church of Holy Innocents' built next door in 1877. On the left in the picture is the teacher's house and on the right, just visible beyond the main gable, is the extension built in 1872. The school was closed in 1934 when Rokesly Infants' School opened nearby. Much of the building, including the belfry was demolished but the schoolroom remained. After suitable conversion it was re-opened in 1981 as the headquarters of the Hornsey Historical Society.

Tottenham Lane, Hornsey

TOTTENHAM LANE, c.1910

Tottenham Lane is an ancient route connecting Crouch End and Hornsey with Wood Green and Tottenham. The Hope and Anchor public house (top left) replaced an earlier tavern on the site at the end of the 19th century as the area began to fill up with terraced housing. Millman Terrace (extreme right) is dated 1889. The trees on the left are in the grounds of Elmcroft and The Old Chestnuts, the latter a doctor's house. Before 1939 this site was to become a commercial garage and in 1955 a motor-car dealers. The public house, Millman Terrace and the other parade (right) remain today.

HORNSEY POLICE FOOTBALL TEAM, 1920

Hornsey Police Station has been in Tottenham Lane since May 1884 when a new building, built to serve the expanding district, began to be operational. This portrait of the team for the 1919-1920 season shows a formidable eleven and three of the officers.

MATTISON ROAD SCHOOL, c.1905

A school photograph of a class at Hornsey Higher Elementary School, Mattison Road. The aim of the Higher Elementary Schools was to provide an advanced education for able children after they had completed their elementary course, at a cost of 6*d* weekly, in the days before secondary education was general. The headmaster, Dr. Pigott, is shown in the centre. The school became Hornsey County School in 1906 and the building, adjoining South Harringay Junior School, still survives.

WIGHTMAN ROAD, 1905

On 1st July 1905 the Bishop of London consecrated the chancel, side-chapel, organ chambers and vestries of St. Peter's church in Wightman Road. The clergy from the surrounding parishes robed in the hall adjoining, processed round the church by Lausanne Road, and entered by the west door. The church began in a temporary structure in 1884; this building replaced it in 1897 and suffered extensive damage in the Second World War. In 1977 the parish merged with Christ Church, West Green.

HORNSEY PARISH CHURCH, c.1910

The view looks towards the parish church of St. Mary in Hornsey High Street, from near the still-remaining drinking fountain and horse trough in Hornsey Green. The parish church had been built by the 13th century and the medieval tower, dating in part at least from 1500 AD, still survives, as does the graveyard with memorials dating from the 16th to 19th centuries. The nave in this picture had replaced the medieval nave in 1833 and it survived until 1927 when it was demolished. In 1888 a separate church had been constructed to the east of this church, on the corner of Church Lane and High Street and was in use until 1969 when it too was demolished and St. Mary's Infant School built on the site. The existence of this other church explains the caption 'Old Hornsey Church', which stood unused when this photograph was taken.

CHURCH LANE, c.1915

On the right is the path into St. Mary's churchyard. At this time both the church built in 1888 and the earlier disused church with the medieval tower still stood. Today an infants school is on the site of the 1888 church and only the medieval tower remains of the earlier church. Some 23 houses are listed at this date for the east side of Church Lane (left). Some are dated 1894. In 1891 there had only been six residences, including Ferrestone lodge and other detached properties.

914.

HORNSEY HIGH STREET, c.1904

In the 1880s there had been several old wooden cottages standing by the green, near Eagle Cottage, seen on the extreme left of this photograph. By the 1890s most of them had gone except this one, Jessamine Cottage, which was a shoemaker's, Elijah King's. The premises are seen just before demolition.

HORNSEY. OLD HOUSES, HIGH STREET.

HORNSEY HIGH STREET c.1904

The weatherboarded shops (left) were for long a feature of the High Street, but these were swept away between the wars, with council baths and wash houses built on this site in 1932. The end shop in the photograph is a cycle manufacturer's, meeting a popular need of the time. The drinking fountain and cattle trough in the distance, near The Great Northern Railway Tavern, still survive.

HORNSEY HIGH STREET, c.1912

The view looks east towards The Great Northern Railway Tavern of 1896 (left) and St. Mary's parish church. The tram lines were laid out by 1905 when a service began between Turnpike Lane and the foot of Muswell Hill.

HORNSEY HIGH STREET, c.1905

The view looks east, with the white jacketed barman (right) standing outside The Three Compasses. This public house was rebuilt in 1896 on the site of a Georgian inn of the same name and still exists. Opposite, on the left, the terrace of shops also remains, although the pawnbroker's sign of three brass balls has gone.

ACKNOWLEDGEMENTS

All the postcards in this publication have been selected from the collection of Dick Whetstone.

Editing by Ken Gay, honorary chairman of Hornsey Historical Society.
Additional editing and marketing by Steve Benz.

Abbreviation used: c. — circa.

Hornsey Historical Society welcomes new members. Its programme includes a monthly illustrated lecture by an outside speaker at 8 p.m. on the second Wednesday of each month (except August) at Hornsey Central Library, Haringey Park, Crouch End N8. In addition it arranges walks, social events, coach outings and visits to places of historical interest. At its headquarters it runs exhibitions, maintains an archive and other facilities available to the public, and sells it publications which range from booklets to postcards and reprinted Ordnance Survey maps of earlier periods. Applications for membership should be made to the Membership Secretary, The Old Schoolhouse, 136 Tottenham Lane, N8 7EL (no phone). Callers are welcome on Thursdays (10 a.m.—noon), Fridays (10 a.m.—noon) and Saturdays (10 a.m.—4 p.m.).